ESCAPE *from* WITHIN

Messages of Hope, Strength, and Spiritual Breakthrough

RATONDREA O'NEAL

Escape From Within: Messages of Hope,
Strength, and Spiritual Breakthrough

Complete Edition

ISBN: 979-8-9930717-0-1

Book Design & Layout by:

Dedication

I dedicate this book to three extraordinary women who have profoundly shaped my life: my mother, my mentor, and my friend.

To my beloved mother, **Veronica Elizabeth Thomas Shaw**, whose strength and love are my foundation. You are not only my mother but my closest friend and my greatest supporter. Your wisdom and unwavering faith continue to inspire me daily. I am blessed to call you, my mother.

"Her children arise and call her blessed; her husband also, and he praises her." Proverbs 31:28 (NIV)

To **Evangelist Rhudine Poole (aka Mother Neneh),** my spiritual mentor and dear friend, you always see me through the eyes of God. Your prayers, guidance, and love are a constant source of strength. Your influence on my life is immeasurable.

"She speaks with wisdom, and faithful instruction is on her tongue." Proverbs 31:26 (NIV)

To the beloved **Sis Connie Jackson**, whose wisdom was both comfort and a guide. Though she is no longer with us, her legacy of compassion and insight continues to resonate in my heart. She listened without judgment and poured wisdom into me, leaving an eternal mark on my life.

"Honor her for all that her hands have done and let her works bring her praise at the city gate." Proverbs 31:31 (NIV)

Each of you touches my heart in ways words cannot fully express, and it is with love and gratitude that I dedicate this book to you.

"Put on the full armor of God, so that you can take your stand against the devil's schemes." Ephesians 6:11 (NIV)

At twelve, God gave me everything I needed to navigate life, and this scripture has guided me ever since.

About this Book

Escape From Within: Messages of Hope, Strength, and Spiritual Breakthrough is a twelve-month devotional series God has placed on my heart to share. Each chapter follows a prayerful structure: an Opening Prayer, a personal or biblical story, the core teaching, reflection questions, a monthly challenge, and Closing Scriptures.

This devotional is designed to be read one chapter per month, giving you time to reflect, apply, and live out the message before moving to the next. At the end of each section, you will be tasked to commit to the principle. Each week, document your Wins and how you have applied the teaching.

You will also find QR codes at the beginning of each chapter that link to brief audio highlights, allowing you to engage the chapter's main points in a concise audio form.

The goal of this book is not simply to inspire but to activate: to help you move from hearing the Word to living the Word. My prayer is that you will encounter God's voice, His direction, and His encouragement in a deeply personal way as you journey through these pages.

How To Use This Devotional

This devotional is designed for a one-year journey. Use one chapter per month so there's space to reflect and apply.

Suggested monthly application:

- **Week 1** – Read & Pray: Read the chapter, pray the Opening Prayer, and underline one 'Point' sentence.
- **Week 2** – Reflect & Journal: Answer 2-3 Reflection Questions and write your weekly Win.
- **Week 3** – Act & Serve: Do the Monthly Challenge and capture a Win.
- **Week 4** – Testify & Review: Share your testimony with a friend/ small group and record your Win.

Listen to the audio message for each chapter:

- Print: Scan the QR code or enter the short link
- eBook/PDF: tap the code

My Wins pages: Sign the monthly commitment and note a Win each week.

Small groups: Read the Point aloud, pick two Reflection Questions, commit to one action, and pray together.

What you will need: A Bible (NIV/your preference), pen, and a journal.

Introduction

When I was in my early twenties, God placed a desire in my heart to write a book, *Escape from Within*. Although life steered me in different directions, I never let go of that dream. Over the years, I faced heart failure, health scares, a flooded house, a failed marriage, and countless struggles. But through it all, God remained faithful. He never left me.

I stand today, alive and well, despite the challenges I faced. My children are thriving, and my heart is healed. This devotional series is not just a collection of teachings; it is a testimony of God's grace and faithfulness in the midst of trials.

When I was twelve, God gave me a scripture that became a cornerstone of my faith: **"Put on the full armor of God, so that you can take your stand against the devil's schemes" (Ephesians 6:11, NIV)**. At that time, I did not understand the depth of the scripture, but God had already planted in me the tools I needed for life's battles.

The number twelve has always been significant to me, symbolizing spiritual completeness. Just as God gave me that scripture at twelve, He has given me twelve devotions to share. These teachings reflect His perfect timing and divine order. My prayer is that you will embrace these teachings over the next twelve months and allow God's word to strengthen you for whatever comes your way.

Contents

PART TWO

PART ONE

Chapter One

As we begin this journey, it is important to remember that God has already placed you in the driver's seat of His purpose. In Chapter One, we will explore what it means to be God's First Choice and how to start your spiritual engine with confidence, knowing that God has equipped you for the road ahead. Let's begin the drive toward discovering your purpose.

 Scan the QR Code or enter the link to listen to the audio message.

https://youtu.be/44IDq3UOQ0U

1

God's First Choice: Start Your Engine and Drive in Purpose

Start your engine. Drive in purpose. Move in faith.

Scripture Focus: 1 Samuel 16:1, 6-7, 11-13 (NIV)

OPENING TRANSITION

As you step into this first month of the journey, remember that the way you start sets the tone for the road ahead. Before we can discuss fueling or even navigating, we must understand that God has already chosen us to be in the driver's seat of His calling. That truth is where our journey begins.

OPENING PRAYER

Heavenly Father, we thank You for this moment to gather in Your name. Lord, help me to represent You. Remove distractions, silence every lie, and let Your presence be felt. Father, use me as Your vessel. Prepare every heart to hear Your voice. Anoint this message; let it break yokes, build confidence, and remind us that we are chosen, called, and capable. Use this word to shift perspectives and revive purpose. In Jesus' name, Amen.

INTRODUCTION

This month, our focus is "God's First Choice." In 1 Samuel 16, the prophet Samuel is sent to anoint Israel's next king. David, the youngest son, is out tending sheep. He was not even invited to the lineup of candidates. Yet God chooses him, reminding Samuel:

"People look at the outward appearance, but the Lord looks at the heart." 1 Samuel 16:7 (NIV)

David was not man's obvious choice, but he was God's. Just like David, you may feel unseen, underestimated, or unqualified. But your obedience, faithfulness, and readiness make you the one God chooses.

PERSONAL STORY

I remember applying for a position that seemed far beyond my qualifications. On paper, I was not the "right" choice. But as I prayed, I heard God whisper, *"I'm the One who chooses."* I walked into the interview leaning fully on Him, and not only did I get the job, but it became a stepping stone to the work I do now. God's choice is about His purpose, not human credentials.

That experience reminded me of a scene that plays out like a living parable. Picture a man standing in his driveway each morning, faced with a choice between two very different cars.

THE STORY

There was a man who, every morning, faced a choice. In his driveway sat two cars: a sleek, black luxury car with chrome rims, leather seats, touchscreen dash, spotless engine; and a rough-looking car with peeling paint, dim headlight, torn seats, stained floors, a noisy engine held together with duct tape, zip ties, and a whole lot of faith. Each morning, he went to the luxury car first. He would press the push-to-start button, but nothing happened. Frustrated, he would turn to the rough car, insert the key, and …Vroom! It started instantly. It wasn't pretty, but it got him to work every single day.

THE POINT

God is not impressed by outer appearance or polish. He looks for the one who starts when He turns the key. You might feel worn, patched together by grace, tired from life's miles, but if your heart responds when He calls, you are His choice. Just like David, you may not look "qualified" in the world's eyes, but under the hood, your worship runs, your prayer life cranks, and your obedience still moves forward.

TRANSITION TO CORE TEACHING

So how do we stay "start-ready" when God turns the key? Let's look at the DRIVE principle, which outlines five ways to keep your spiritual engine running strong and aligned with His purpose.

CORE TEACHING - THE D.R.I.V.E. PRINCIPLE

D – Dependable: Be the one God can count on. Not perfect, but present. Ready to go when He calls. (1 Corinthians 4:2)

R – Ready: Live in a posture of expectation and obedience. Keep your spiritual engine tuned. (Luke 12:35)

I – Intentional: Live on purpose, with purpose. Do not drift - drive. (Proverbs 4:25)

V – Vessel: You carry God's glory. What matters most is what He has placed inside you. (2 Corinthians 4:7)

E – Empowered: Not by your own strength, but by the Holy Spirit. That is your fuel. (Acts 1:8)

Principles like these are not meant to stay on the page. They are meant to show up on your daily walk. Let's pause and see where your own "engine" might need tuning.

REFLECTION QUESTIONS

1. When have you felt "overlooked" but later realized you were chosen by God?

2. What does it mean for you to "start when God turns the key"?

3. Which DRIVE quality do you most need to strengthen right now?

4. How do you keep your spiritual engine tuned and ready?

5. Who in your life could you encourage this week by telling them they are God's first choice?

Now that you have reflected, it is time to take action, because readiness is proven in movement.

MONTHLY CHALLENGE

For the next 30 days:

-   Begin each morning with a prayer of readiness: "Lord, I am here. Send me."

-   Act promptly when God prompts you to speak, serve, or step out.

-   Document in a journal the moments you responded immediately to His call. Then review and give thanks.

CLOSING SCRIPTURES TO MEDITATE ON

"The Lord looks at the heart." (1 Samuel 16:7)

"For I know the plans I have for you…" (Jeremiah 29:11)

"He who began a good work in you…" (Philippians 1:6)

"All things work together for good…" (Romans 8:28)

TAKE IT FURTHER

This week, spend 15 minutes journaling about a time you felt overlooked but later realized God had chosen you for something special. End your journaling session by praying over your current season, asking God to open your eyes to the opportunities He has placed in front of you today.

D.R.I.V.E. Principle

This is where what you have read becomes how you live. Over the next four weeks, record your wins as proof of God's work in and through you.

Small victories build lasting transformation. Recording them creates a testimony you can return to for encouragement. Each week, note progress in the Reflection, Challenge, and Take It Further activities.

This month, I commit to living out **D.R.I.V.E.** (Dependable, Ready, Intentional, a Vessel, and Empowered).

Signature: _____ Date: _____

WEEK 1:

Reflection Question Win: _____

30-Day Challenge Win: _____

Take It Further Win: _____

WEEK 2:

Reflection Question Win: _____

30-Day Challenge Win: _____

Take It Further Win: _____

WEEK 3:

Reflection Question Win: _____

30-Day Challenge Win: _____

Take It Further Win: _____

WEEK 4:

Reflection Question Win: _____

30-Day Challenge Win: _____

Take It Further Win: _____

Chapter Two

Being chosen is only the beginning. Once you know God has placed you in the driver's seat, the next question is: How will you keep moving forward without running out of strength? Just like a car cannot run on an empty tank, your spiritual life requires the right fuel. In the next chapter, we'll explore how to lift the nozzle, choose the right grade, and fuel your faith for the journey ahead.

 Scan the QR Code or enter the link to listen to the audio message.

https://youtu.be/oyrKrnsPE9s

CHAPTER

2

Lift the Nozzle, Select the Grade, Begin Fueling

Don't run on empty—refuel your faith today.

Scripture Focus: Philippians 4:13; Isaiah 40:31; John 15:5 (NIV)

OPENING TRANSITION

You have turned the key and answered God's call. Now you need the strength to keep moving. Like a driver pulling up to a gas station before a long journey, this is the time to refuel your spirit, so you do not stall out along the way. God's fueling station never runs out, but you must be intentional about pulling in, lifting the nozzle, and filling up with His power.

OPENING PRAYER

Father, thank You for being our constant source of strength and provision. Today, open our hearts to receive Your word, open our minds to understand Your ways, and open our spirits to be filled with Your power. Help us to refuel in Your presence and run the race set before us with endurance. In Jesus' name, Amen.

INTRODUCTION

Life will drain you. Demands pull from every side, and before you know it, you are running on empty. But God has given us a divine fueling station, His presence. Just as a car cannot run without gas, we cannot operate at our best without regular spiritual refueling. In this chapter, we learn how to lift the nozzle, select the right grade, and begin fueling our faith for the journey ahead.

PERSONAL STORY

I will never forget a season when I poured myself into ministry, work, and family without stopping to rest in God's presence. I was running, but my spiritual tank was on fumes. It was not until I took a weekend to step away, pray, and worship that I felt His strength pour back into me. That moment **reminded me that, just as a car needs fuel, I cannot keep going without His power.**

That moment in my life brought to mind a vivid picture of how we sometimes show up in the right place but still leave empty.

THE STORY

Picture yourself pulling into a gas station with the fuel light blinking red. You stop, get out, lift the nozzle, and choose the grade your car needs. Then you fill up and continue with renewed strength. Spiritually, many of us have been driving with that warning light on. God invites us to pull in, refuel, and keep going, not on fumes, but on His power.

THE POINT

Just as you choose the fuel for your car, you choose the quality of what you put in your spirit. Not all fuel is good fuel. When we lift the nozzle, in prayer, worship, and the Word, and allow the Holy Spirit to fill us, we receive the energy, peace, and clarity to keep moving forward.

TRANSITION TO CORE TEACHING

So, how do we ensure our spiritual tank stays full and ready for the journey? The FUEL principle gives us four practical ways to stay filled with God's power.

CORE TEACHING - THE F.U.E.L. PRINCIPLE

F – Focus on God: Keep your attention fixed on Him, not your distractions. (Hebrews 12:2)

U – Understand Your Source: You cannot sustain yourself. He is the vine; you are the branch. (John 15:5)

E – Engage in Spiritual Discipline: Prayer, fasting, worship, and the Word keep your tank full. (Joshua 1:8)

L – Let the Holy Spirit Lead: When He directs your steps, you will never stall. (Romans 8:14)

Before we move forward, let's pause and take a closer look at how this truth applies to your life personally.

REFLECTION QUESTIONS

1. What warning lights have been showing up in your life lately?

2. Where have you been running empty?

3. Which "grade" of fuel have you been putting into your spirit, and does it align with God's Word?

4. How can you make more time to refuel daily?

5. What is one change you can make this week to protect your spiritual fuel supply?

Now that you have reflected, let's turn your answers into intentional action this month.

MONTHLY CHALLENGE

For the next 30 days:

- Start each day with 10 minutes of uninterrupted prayer or worship before checking your phone.

- Read one chapter of Scripture daily and note one application.

- End each day with gratitude, thanking God for how He "filled your tank."

CLOSING SCRIPTURES TO MEDITATE ON

"I can do all this through Him who gives me strength." (Philippians 4:13)

"Those who hope in the Lord will renew their strength…" (Isaiah 40:31)

"Apart from me, you can do nothing." (John 15:5)

TAKE IT FURTHER

Choose one of this week's devotional or worship times to do outdoors, at a park, on your porch, or during a quiet walk. Let the change of scenery remind you of the fresh strength and perspective God wants to pour into you.

F.U.E.L. Principle

This is where what you have read becomes how you live. Over the next four weeks, record your wins as proof of God's work in and through you.

Small victories build lasting transformation. Recording them creates a testimony you can return to for encouragement. Each week, note progress in the Reflection, Challenge, and Take It Further activities.

This month, I commit to living out **F.U.E.L.** (Focus on God, Understand Your Source, Engage in Spiritual Discipline, and Let the Holy Spirit Lead).

Signature: _____ Date: _____

WEEK 1:

Reflection Question Win: _____

30-Day Challenge Win: _____

Take It Further Win: _____

WEEK 2:

Reflection Question Win: _____

30-Day Challenge Win: _____

Take It Further Win: _____

WEEK 3:

Reflection Question Win: _____

30-Day Challenge Win: _____

Take It Further Win: _____

WEEK 4:

Reflection Question Win: _____

30-Day Challenge Win: _____

Take It Further Win: _____

Chapter Three

When your tank is full, you can travel farther and face obstacles with renewed energy. But what happens when life's noise tries to block your connection to God? In the next chapter, we will talk about how even when the lines on earth are muted, Heaven's line remains wide open.

 Scan the QR Code or enter the link to listen to the audio message.

https://youtu.be/-0oNMPF2RKE

3

Muted Lines, Open Heaven

Silence doesn't mean separation—
Heaven is still speaking.

Scripture Focus: Psalm 34:17; Isaiah 65:24; Jeremiah 33:3 (NIV)

OPENING TRANSITION

When your spirit is fueled and ready for the journey, communication with your Navigator becomes essential. But what happens when you feel like your prayers are bouncing back, or your voice is drowned out by the noise of life? In this chapter, we will see that even when it feels like your words are muted, Heaven is still tuned in.

OPENING PRAYER

Lord, we thank You that no matter where we are or what we face, You always hear us. You know our hearts even when we cannot speak the words. Remind us that Heaven's line is always open and helps us stay connected to You in prayer—in our words, in our silence, and in our tears. In Jesus' name, Amen.

INTRODUCTION

There are moments in life when our voices feel muted by pain, fear, or the sense that no one understands. Yet even in our silence, God hears us. The line to Heaven is never busy, never disconnected, and never muted. He hears your whispers, your sighs, your heartbeat.

PERSONAL STORY

I have had days when I could not form the words to pray. All I could do was sit in His presence with tears streaming down my face. I thought my silence might mean my prayer was incomplete, but later, God answered in ways that proved He had heard every unspoken plea.

That experience made me think of a moment we have all had someone saying, "You're on mute!" This perfectly pictures how prayer can feel sometimes.

THE STORY

Think about being on a video call, passionately sharing your thoughts, only for someone to say, "You're on mute!" Life can feel like that. But with God, there is no mute button, no poor signal, no bad timing. Prayer is the original wireless connection, unlimited, secure, and available 24/7.

THE POINT

"Before they call, I will answer; while they are still speaking, I will hear." Isaiah 65:24 (NIV)

You can pour out your heart to Him in full sentences, in a quiet whisper, or in complete silence, and He still receives every word. Silent prayers carry just as much power as spoken ones.

TRANSITION TO CORE TEACHING

So how do we keep our prayer line to Heaven open, even when life gets noisy? The OPEN principle gives us four ways to stay connected to God's heart.

CORE TEACHING - THE O.P.E.N. PRINCIPLE

O – Ongoing Connection: Stay connected to God at all times; do not hang up. (1 Thessalonians 5:17)

P – Prayer in All Forms: Pray with your words, with your worship, and with your tears. (Romans 8:26)

E – Expect an Answer: God promises to respond when you call. (Jeremiah 33:3)

N – Never Doubt His Hearing: Even when it feels quiet, Heaven hears. (Psalm 34:17)

Let's bring this from principle to practice. Use these prompts to check your connection with God right now.

REFLECTION QUESTIONS

1. When was a time you felt like no one was listening, but you knew God heard you?

2. How can you keep your "line to Heaven" open daily?

3. In what ways have you prayed silently but still experienced an answer?

4. Which part of the OPEN principle do you need to strengthen?

5. Who in your life needs the reminder that God hears even their unspoken prayers?

Now, turn your reflections into a simple rhythm you can live out this month.

MONTHLY CHALLENGE

For the next 30 days:

- Dedicate a few minutes each day to silent prayer.
- Record situations where God answered prayers you never spoke aloud.
- Share a testimony about a time God answered a quiet prayer.

CLOSING SCRIPTURES TO MEDITATE ON

"The righteous cry out, and the Lord hears them; he delivers them from all their troubles." (Psalm 34:17)

"Before they call, I will answer; while they are still speaking, I will hear." (Isaiah 65:24)

"Call to me and I will answer you and tell you great and unsearchable things you do not know." (Jeremiah 33:3)

TAKE IT FURTHER

This week, set aside one evening to sit in God's presence without speaking. Play soft worship music or simply enjoy the silence. Pay attention to the thoughts, scriptures, or images He brings to mind. Write them in your journal as reminders that Heaven is always listening.

MY WINS THIS MONTH
O.P.E.N. Principle

This is where what you have read becomes how you live. Over the next four weeks, record your wins as proof of God's work in and through you.

Small victories build lasting transformation. Recording them creates a testimony you can return to for encouragement. Each week, note progress in the Reflection, Challenge, and Take It Further activities.

This month, I commit to living out **O.P.E.N.** (Ongoing Connection, Prayer in All Forms, Expect an Answer, and Never Doubt His Hearing).

Signature: _____ Date: _____

WEEK 1:

Reflection Question Win: _____

30-Day Challenge Win: _____

Take It Further Win: _____

WEEK 2:

Reflection Question Win: _____

30-Day Challenge Win: _____

Take It Further Win: _____

WEEK 3:

Reflection Question Win: _____

30-Day Challenge Win: _____

Take It Further Win: _____

WEEK 4:

Reflection Question Win: _____

30-Day Challenge Win: _____

Take It Further Win: _____

Chapter Four

When you know the line to Heaven is always open, you cannot help but listen to His instructions. But sometimes those instructions come with urgency. God does not just want you connected; He wants you awake. In the next chapter, we will discover why your assignment cannot wait another day.

🔊 Scan the QR Code or enter the link to listen to the audio message.

https://youtu.be/w26na60DMrk

CHAPTER

4

Wake Up! Wake Up! Your Assignment is Waiting!

The alarm has sounded—your purpose is calling.

Scripture Focus: Romans 13:11-12; Ephesians 5:14; 2 Timothy 4:5 (NIV)

OPENING TRANSITION

Knowing God hears your every prayer should give you confidence to listen and respond quickly. But if the line to Heaven is open and we still do not move, the message gets lost in delay. God does not just want you connected. He wants you to stay awake, alert, and ready to act.

OPENING PRAYER

Father, awaken our hearts to the call You have placed on our lives. Remove distractions, discouragement, and delay. Stir up our gifts, reignite our passion, and give us courage to walk in the assignments You have entrusted to us. In Jesus' name, Amen.

INTRODUCTION

"The hour has already come for you to wake up from your slumber, because our salvation is nearer now than when we first believed." Romans 13:11 (NIV)

God calls, nudges, and prompts, but we often delay, thinking we will get to it "later." Yet later often becomes never. This is your wake-up call.

PERSONAL STORY

I recall a time when I felt God nudging me to reach out to someone I hadn't spoken to in years. I kept putting it off, telling myself I would do it tomorrow. Weeks later, I learned they had been going through a deep personal crisis during that time. I will never forget the heaviness I felt, knowing my delay meant missing a moment to encourage them. I learned from that experience that **delayed obedience is often a lost opportunity**.

That experience made me think of a simple picture that illustrates how delay steals moments, much like an alarm you keep snoozing.

THE STORY

A man set his alarm for an important meeting. The alarm rang. Again, snooze. He arrived late and missed his moment. Spiritually, many of us live like that. God invites us to act now.

THE POINT

"Wake up, sleeper, rise from the dead, and Christ will shine on you." Ephesians 5:14 (NIV)

Your assignment is time sensitive. Every day you delay is a day someone goes without the encouragement, guidance, or help you were meant to provide.

TRANSITION TO CORE TEACHING

So how do we stay spiritually awake and ready to respond when God calls? The ALARM principle gives us five ways to avoid hitting the snooze button on our purpose.

CORE TEACHING - THE A.L.A.R.M. PRINCIPLE

A – Awareness: Be alert to God's voice and the opportunities He presents. (1 Peter 5:8)

L – Listen: Do not ignore the nudge of the Holy Spirit—respond when He calls. (John 10:27)

A – Action: Faith without works is dead. Move when God says move. (James 2:17)

R – Resist Delay: Procrastination is one of the enemy's silent weapons. Resist it. (Proverbs 6:9-11)

M – Mission-Minded: Keep your eyes on the assignment, not the distractions. (2 Timothy 4:5)

Let's pause and identify where we might be spiritually dozing and where God is calling for an immediate response.

REFLECTION QUESTIONS

1. What "spiritual snooze buttons" have you been pressing lately?

2. How has delay impacted your obedience in the past?

3. Which part of the ALARM principle do you need to strengthen?

4. What is one immediate step you can take toward your God-given assignment this week?

5. Who is waiting for you to wake up and act?

Faith wakes up and moves.

Turn what you noticed into decisive action this month.

MONTHLY CHALLENGE

For the next 30 days:

- Pray daily: "Lord, I am awake and ready. Show me my assignment today."

- Identify one area where you have delayed obedience and take action this week.

- Keep a journal of "wake-up moments" and your responses.

CLOSING SCRIPTURES TO MEDITATE ON

"The hour has already come for you to wake up from your slumber." (Romans 13:11)

"Wake up, sleeper, rise from the dead, and Christ will shine on you." (Ephesians 5:14)

"Keep your head in all situations… do the work of an evangelist." (2 Timothy 4:5)

TAKE IT FURTHER

Identify one task, conversation, or step of obedience you have been putting off. Commit to doing it within the next 48 hours. As soon as you complete it, take a few minutes to thank God for the opportunity and ask Him for your next assignment.

A.L.A.R.M. Principle

This is where what you have read becomes how you live. Over the next four weeks, record your wins as proof of God's work in and through you.

Small victories build lasting transformation. Recording them creates a testimony you can return to for encouragement. Each week, note progress in the Reflection, Challenge, and Take It Further activities.

This month, I commit to living out **A.L.A.R.M.** (Awareness, Listen, Action, Resist Delay, and Mission-Minded).

Signature: _____ Date: _____

WEEK 1:

Reflection Question Win: _____

30-Day Challenge Win: _____

Take It Further Win: _____

WEEK 2:

Reflection Question Win: _____

30-Day Challenge Win: _____

Take It Further Win: _____

WEEK 3:

Reflection Question Win: _____

30-Day Challenge Win: _____

Take It Further Win: _____

WEEK 4:

Reflection Question Win: _____

30-Day Challenge Win: _____

Take It Further Win: _____

Chapter Five

Once you are awake and ready, the next step is to walk, step by step, in faith. Not the kind of faith that stays in words, but the kind that moves, trusts, and transforms even the messiest seasons of life into something beautiful. That is where we are headed next.

 Scan the QR Code or enter the link to listen to the audio message.

https://youtu.be/pV4P7Qujhlo

CHAPTER

5

Walk by Faith, Don't Just Talk: Turn Manure into Something Beautiful

*Your manure moment might just be
the making of your miracle.*

Scripture Focus: 2 Corinthians 5:7; James 2:17; Romans 8:28 (NIV)

OPENING TRANSITION

Being awake to your assignment is only the beginning. Once your spiritual eyes are open, God calls you to move forward in faith, even when the path is messy, unclear, or filled with obstacles. True faith does not just talk; it walks, even when the ground is covered in what looks like waste.

OPENING PRAYER

Lord, teach us to live in the reality of Your promises. Remove fear, doubt, and hesitation. Help us trust Your process, even when it is not pretty and remember that You can turn life's messes into miracles. In Jesus' name, Amen.

INTRODUCTION

We have heard the phrase "walk by faith, not by sight," but sometimes our actions often don't align with our words. Faith is more than a declaration. It is a daily decision to trust God when the road is messy, unclear, and uncomfortable.

"Faith by itself, if it is not accompanied by action, is dead." James 2:17 (NIV)

PERSONAL STORY

I think back to a season when everything seemed to go wrong at once - unexpected bills, health scares, and disappointments piling up. I felt buried. But as I continued to pray and take small steps of faith, I realized that God was using that season to grow me. What I thought was burying me was actually planting me.

That season taught me a lesson I will never forget. One that came to life in a simple story but carried a deep spiritual truth.

THE STORY - THE BIRD AND THE SNOW
(Traditional Moral Story – Author Unknown)

A small bird, freezing in winter, fell into a field. A cow dropped manure on it. Disgusted at first, the bird soon warmed and began to sing. A cat, hearing the song, dug the bird out and ate it.

Moral: Not everyone who drops something unpleasant on you is your enemy, and not everyone who digs you out is your friend. Sometimes the very thing you think is ruining you is the thing God is using to save you.

THE POINT

"And we know that in all things God works for the good of those who love him…" Romans 8:28 (NIV)

Life can be messy "manure" moments. But faith trusts that God can turn the smelliest seasons into fertile ground for growth.

TRANSITION TO CORE TEACHING

So how do we keep walking when the road is covered in challenges? The FAITH principle outlines five steps to move from talking faith to living it.

CORE TEACHING - THE F.A.I.T.H. PRINCIPLE

F – Focus on God's Promise: Do not get distracted by what you see - hold on to what He said. (Hebrews 10:23)

A – Act on His Word: Faith moves. Take the next step, even if you cannot see the whole path. (Matthew 14:29)

I – Ignore the Naysayers: Some people will not understand your journey. Keep going anyway. (Nehemiah 6:3)

T – Trust His Timing: Delay does not mean denial. (Ecclesiastes 3:1)

H – Hold Your Peace: Stay calm in the process. God is working -even in the manure. (Exodus 14:14)

Before you move on, pause and locate where your faith needs to start walking right now.

REFLECTION QUESTIONS

1. What is one "manure moment" in your life that God later used for good?

2. Which part of the FAITH principle do you struggle with most?

3. What tangible step will move you from "talking faith" to "walking faith" this week?

4. Who can you encourage with a testimony of God turning mess into beauty?

5. What scripture will you stand on when circumstances seem hopeless?

Now turn those insights into simple, steady practices this month.

MONTHLY CHALLENGE

For the next 30 days:

- Identify one area where you have been speaking faith but not walking in it and take one concrete step forward.

- Keep a "Faith Journal," recording how God shows up in situations that seemed hopeless.

- Share one testimony this month with someone who needs encouragement.

CLOSING SCRIPTURES TO MEDITATE ON

"For we live by faith, not by sight." (2 Corinthians 5:7)

"Faith by itself, if it is not accompanied by action, is dead." (James 2:17)

"In all things God works for the good of those who love Him." (Romans 8:28)

TAKE IT FURTHER

Write down one current situation in your life that feels like a "manure moment." Each day this week, pray over it and declare a scripture from this chapter. Watch for ways God begins to turn that situation into fertile ground for growth.

F.A.I.T.H. Principle

This is where what you have read becomes how you live. Over the next four weeks, record your wins as proof of God's work in and through you.

Small victories build lasting transformation. Recording them creates a testimony you can return to for encouragement. Each week, note progress in the Reflection, Challenge, and Take It Further activities.

This month, I commit to living out **F.A.I.T.H.** (Focus on God's Promise, Act on His Word, Ignore the Naysayers, Trust His timing, and Hold Your Peace).

Signature: _____ Date: _____

WEEK 1:

Reflection Question Win: _____

30-Day Challenge Win: _____

Take It Further Win: _____

WEEK 2:

Reflection Question Win: _____

30-Day Challenge Win: _____

Take It Further Win: _____

WEEK 3:

Reflection Question Win: _____

30-Day Challenge Win: _____

Take It Further Win: _____

WEEK 4:

Reflection Question Win: _____

30-Day Challenge Win: _____

Take It Further Win: _____

Chapter Six

Faith that walks will eventually lead you to places God has specifically chosen for you, sometimes across the street, sometimes across the globe. The next chapter reminds us that we are not just saved to sit still; we are sent with purpose, just as Jesus was sent by the Father.

 Scan the QR Code or enter the link to listen to the audio message.

https://youtu.be/5YNPLdn1XI8

CHAPTER

6

Sent by the Father

You weren't sent by accident—you were sent by the Father.

You are chosen. You are called. You are sent.

Scripture Focus: John 20:21, Matthew 28:19-20, Psalm 68:5 (NIV)

OPENING TRANSITION

When you walk by faith, God does not just lead you into personal break-through. He equips you for a mission. Faith in action naturally moves you into being *sent*. Every step you take in obedience positions you to carry His message of hope, love, and redemption into the lives of others.

OPENING PRAYER

Heavenly Father, thank You for sending Your Son to save us and for sending us into the world with Your message of hope. Help us embrace our assignment, walk boldly in our calling, and trust that Your presence goes with us wherever You send us. In Jesus' name, Amen.

INTRODUCTION

Some celebrate Father's Day with joy; others carry a mix of emotions. Regardless of our experiences, we rest in the truth that we have a perfect Father in Heaven. Jesus said, "As the Father has sent me, I am sending you." John 20:21 (NIV)

That means every believer is on a mission. Whether we feel qualified or not, God chooses us, equips us, and sends us.

PERSONAL STORY

I used to think being "sent" meant traveling across the world. But one day, God reminded me that He was sending me into my workplace, my neighborhood, and even my own family. That shift changed everything. I began to view each interaction as a chance to represent Him.

That shift naturally points to a biblical moment that captures what it means to be sent.

THE STORY - THE WOMAN AT THE WELL (JOHN 4)

The Samaritan woman came for water but left with a mission. She came empty. Jesus filled her. She came thirsty. He quenched her soul. She came broken; she left as a messenger. She had no title, pulpit, or license. She had a story, and that story became her ministry.

THE POINT

When you have met the Father through the Son, your life becomes a testimony. You do not need to be a pastor or missionary to be "sent." Your assignment might be in your home, workplace, community, or anywhere across the globe.

TRANSITION TO CORE TEACHING

So how do we live sent every day, no matter where God places us? The FATHER principle shows us six ways to walk in our mission with confidence and purpose.

CORE TEACHING - THE F.A.T.H.E.R. PRINCIPLE

F – Faithful: God never sends us alone; His faithfulness goes with us. (Lamentations 3:23)

A – Available: He uses those who say, "Here I am." (Isaiah 6:8)

T – Teacher: He instructs and corrects those He loves. (Hebrews 12:6)

H – Healer: He sends us with a message that restores hearts. (Isaiah 53:5)

E – Example: Jesus modeled servant leadership for us to follow. (John 13:15)

R – Redeemer: Our mission is rooted in the redemption we have experienced. (Psalm 107:2)

Before you move on, pause and name where you sense God is actively sending you right now.

REFLECTION QUESTIONS

1. Where do you sense God sending you in this season?

2. Which part of the FATHER principle do you need to lean into most right now?

3. How can you share your testimony in a way that points people to Christ?

4. Who might be waiting for you to step into your assignment?

5. What fears or excuses do you need to release to fully obey God's sending?

Turn those insights into simple, steady action over the next month.

MONTHLY CHALLENGE

For the next 30 days:

- Pray each morning: "Lord, I am willing. Send me."

- Look for one opportunity each week to intentionally share encouragement or your testimony with others.

- Take a step in an area where you have hesitated to obey God's direction.

CLOSING SCRIPTURES TO MEDITATE ON

"As the Father has sent me, I am sending you." (John 20:21)

"Go and make disciples of all nations…" (Matthew 28:19-20)

"A Father to the fatherless, a defender of widows, is God in his holy dwelling." (Psalm 68:5)

TAKE IT FURTHER

This week, pray for God to highlight one person you can encourage or help. Be intentional about acting on His prompting, whether it is through a conversation, a small gift, or simply listening. Write about the experience and how God used it in both your life and theirs.

F.A.T.H.E.R. Principle

This is where what you have read becomes how you live. Over the next four weeks, record your wins as proof of God's work in and through you.

Small victories build lasting transformation. Recording them creates a testimony you can return to for encouragement. Each week, note progress in the Reflection, Challenge, and Take It Further activities.

This month, I commit to living out **F.A.T.H.E.R.** (Faithful, Available, Teacher, Healer, Example, and Redeemer).

Signature: _____ Date: _____

WEEK 1:

Reflection Question Win: _____

30-Day Challenge Win: _____

Take It Further Win: _____

WEEK 2:

Reflection Question Win: _____

30-Day Challenge Win: _____

Take It Further Win: _____

WEEK 3:

Reflection Question Win: _____

30-Day Challenge Win: _____

Take It Further Win: _____

WEEK 4:

Reflection Question Win: _____

30-Day Challenge Win: _____

Take It Further Win: _____

Transition for Part One

This marks the end of the first leg of our journey together. It is only the beginning of the mission God has for you. You have been reminded that you are chosen, fueled, heard, awakened, walking in faith, and sent with purpose. As you step forward, may these truths become more than words on a page - they are your marching orders from Heaven. Part Two will take us deeper into the remaining exhortations, building on the foundation we have laid here. Until then, walk boldly, love deeply, and live sent.

CLOSING SUMMARY AND CALL TO ACTION

As we come to the end of Part One, I encourage you to reflect on the powerful truths we have uncovered together. We have learned to DRIVE with purpose, staying spiritually ready and aligned with God's calling. We have discussed how to FUEL your faith, ensuring you are filled with God's strength for the journey. You have discovered how to keep your communication line open to Heaven through the OPEN principle, even when life feels chaotic. We have also learned how to stay spiritually awake and active through the ALARM principle, which enables us to move from delay to decisive action.

To these foundations, we now add two pillars that shape how you live and lead. We have learned to walk by FAITH, choosing to focus on God's promise, Act on His word, ignore the naysayers, trust His timing, and hold our peace. We have also embraced the sending heart of the FATHER, committing to be faithful, available, teachable under His loving discipline as a teacher, willing to carry His message of healing, following Jesus as our example, and living as witnesses to the redeemer.

Each of these steps is a vital part of your spiritual growth. They help you move from one phase to the next, preparing you for both challenges and victories. This journey is not over. Part Two awaits, inviting you to continue your walk with God and to build on what you have learned so far.

Now it is time to take the next step. You have learned the importance of being dependable and ready through DRIVE, of keeping your spirit focused and empowered through FUEL, of staying connected with God through OPEN, of remaining alert and mission-minded through ALARM, of living by faith in action, and of serving as one sent by the FATHER. These principles are not only for reflection. They are for daily practice.

As you prepare to continue this journey into Part Two, consider these next actions:

1. **Apply** the principles you have learned. Each month, use DRIVE, FUEL, OPEN, ALARM, FAITH, and FATHER to assess where you are and where God is calling you to go.

2. **Share** what you have learned with others. Invite a friend, a family member, or a small group to walk with you. Practice these principles together and celebrate wins along the way.

3. **Stay expectant**. What you have learned is foundational, and there is more to come. In Part Two, we will go deeper, strengthening your daily walk and equipping you for the road ahead.

The road before you is one of continued faith, growth, and transformation. Let your faith lead you to walk in purpose with each step. Let the voice of the Father send you into everyday assignments with courage and love.

Remember this truth. You are chosen. You are empowered by the Holy Spirit. You are ready to continue this journey with Him. Part Two is waiting, and your story of spiritual breakthrough is only beginning.

May you continue to **DRIVE** with purpose, **FUEL** your faith daily, stay **OPEN** to God's voice, live **ALARM** ready, walk by **FAITH**, and follow the sending heart of the **FATHER**.

PART TWO

Chapter Seven

Pause. Breathe. Return. We have learned to start and stay fueled; now we learn to be made whole. You are chosen, fueled, heard, awakened, walking in faith, and sent with purpose. Step into Part Two and place every piece in Jesus' hands.

 Scan the QR Code or enter the link to listen to the audio message.

https://youtu.be/ZpZbYOz33uw

7

Mend On Purpose: From Brokenness to Restoration

Mend on purpose. Heal with faith. Rise restored.

Scripture Focus: Numbers 22:21-35; Proverbs 1:24 (NLT); Nehemiah 1:9; 1 Peter 5:10 (NIV)

OPENING TRANSITION

When your heart stays connected to God, the next step is letting Him repair what life has cracked. Maybe you've felt like Humpty Dumpty, shattered beyond help. But our King specializes in restoration. What initially appears to be a dead end can become a construction zone for renewal.

OPENING PRAYER

Father, thank You that broken does not mean finished. Meet me here. Show me where I need to return, what I need to release, and the next step you are asking me to take. Restore me by Your grace. In Jesus' name, Amen.

INTRODUCTION

There are moments when our souls feel in pieces by grief, by disappointment, and by battles we did not see coming. Brokenness is not always failure; often it is the place where pride ends, and surrender begins. And right there, God meets us; not to discard us, but to rebuild us.

PERSONAL STORY

There were a few times in my life when I felt so miserable I wanted to give up. I felt stuck on a wall, frozen between fear and exhaustion. I believed that if I fell and shattered, no one could help me. In that place, the Lord met me. He did not shame my weakness. He steadied me. Piece by piece, He began to mend what I thought was beyond repair, even using unlikely interruptions to stop my slide and turn me back toward Him.

THE STORY

Picture a car after a fender bender. You do not junk it; you take it to a body shop. Panels are straightened, parts replaced, alignment corrected, and eventually, it is road-ready again. Spiritually, restoration works the same way. God does not throw you away; He brings you into His shop to realign, rebuild, and send you back out stronger. Humpty Dumpty could not be reassembled by the king's horses and men, but our King can and does.

THE POINT

In Numbers 22, Balaam kept pressing forward until God used a donkey to stop him, an *unlikely interruption* that saved his life. Proverbs 1:24 (NLT) warns that ignoring wisdom leads to a fall. But when we turn back, God promises restoration (Nehemiah 1:9). And 1 Peter 5:10 declares that the God of all grace will Himself **restore, confirm, strengthen,** and **establish** you.

TRANSITION TO CORE TEACHING

So, practically, how do we cooperate with God's restoring work this month? Use the MEND principle as your road map to mend on Purpose.

CORE TEACHING -THE M.E.N.D. PRINCIPLE

M – Meet God: Return to Him first. Begin each day by acknowledging His presence and inviting His lead (Nehemiah 1:9).

E – Examine the Cracks: Name the places of strain (habits, lies, patterns, pressures). Wisdom has been calling; where did you ignore it? Proverbs 1:24 (NLT)

N – Name the Promise: Speak Scripture over the broken place. Declare 1 Peter 5:10 or Nehemiah 1:9 daily. God Himself will restore and strengthen you.

D – Do the Next Step: Obedience is the stitch that holds the mend. Make the call, set the boundary, repent, or pause when God puts a "donkey" in your path (cf. Numbers 22).

Before moving on, pause and consider where you are in the MEND principle today.

REFLECTION QUESTIONS

1. Where do you feel cracked—emotionally, spiritually, or relationally?

2. What "warning voice" (Scripture, counsel, conscience) have you been ignoring?

3. Which promise will you "name" over your situation this week (Neh. 1:9 or 1 Pet. 5:10)?

4. What is one courageous, obedient step you can take in the next 24 hours?

5. Who can pray with you and keep you accountable as you heal?

Now that you have reflected, let's turn your answers into intentional action this month. The MEND principle will guide you step by step to mend on purpose.

MONTHLY CHALLENGE

For the next 30 days:

- **Three times a week**: Examine the Cracks. Journal one pattern God is surfacing (worry, pride, isolation, overwork) and counter it with Scripture.

- **Weekly: Do the Next Step**. Choose one concrete act of obedience (apologize, schedule counseling, set a boundary, rest day).

- **End of Month:** Record a brief testimony: "Here's how God began to mend me," and share it with a trusted friend or small group.

CLOSING SCRIPTURES TO MEDITATE ON

"...the God of all grace... will **restore**, **confirm**, **strengthen**, and **establish** you." (1 Peter 5:10)

"If you **return** to Me... I will **gather** you..." (Nehemiah 1:9)

"I called you so often, but you wouldn't come." (Proverbs 1:24 NLT)

"Then the Lord **opened the donkey's mouth**..." (Numbers 22:28)

TAKE IT FURTHER

Hold a small object (a puzzle piece or cracked pottery). As you pray, imagine placing each "piece" into the hands of our King, Jesus. Then take a short Restoration Walk this week with a notebook: list the pieces you are asking God to mend and write one promise beside each. Close with a simple prayer of return and trust.

M.E.N.D. Principle

This is where what you have read becomes how you live. Over the next four weeks, record your wins as proof of God's work in and through you.

Small victories build lasting transformation. Recording them creates a testimony you can return to for encouragement. Each week, note progress in the Reflection, Challenge, and Take It Further activities.

This month, I commit to living out **M.E.N.D.** (Meet God, Examine the Cracks, Name the Promise, and Do the Next Step).

Signature: _____ Date: _____

WEEK 1:

Reflection Question Win: _____

30-Day Challenge Win: _____

Take It Further Win: _____

WEEK 2:

Reflection Question Win: _____

30-Day Challenge Win: _____

Take It Further Win: _____

WEEK 3:

Reflection Question Win: _____

30-Day Challenge Win: _____

Take It Further Win: _____

WEEK 4:

Reflection Question Win: _____

30-Day Challenge Win: _____

Take It Further Win: _____

Chapter Eight

We have let God mend what life cracked; now it is time to move. Restoration prepared our hearts—obedience must move our feet. Chapter 8 calls us to stop keeping God waiting and say "yes" now.

 Scan the QR Code or enter the link to listen to the audio message.

https://youtu.be/IETzu_cOgSY

8

The Delay: Stop Keeping God Waiting

Stop waiting for a sign—God may be waiting for your yes.

Scripture Focus: 2 Corinthians 6:1-2 (NIV); Revelation 3:20 (NIV); Haggai 1:5-7 (NIV); Luke 14:16-20 (NIV)

OPENING TRANSITION

After God mends what is broken, the next step is simple, but costly: move when He speaks. We do not always tell God "No"; we tell Him "Not Yet." But "Not Yet" silently drains momentum and muffles purpose. Today, we end the delay.

OPENING PRAYER

Lord, forgive us for postponing Your presence and purpose. Clear our excuses, reorder our loves, and give us grace to respond today. In Jesus' name - Amen.

INTRODUCTION

Delay feels harmless, one more project, one more season, one more reason. But "delay" compounds. It steals fruit, dulls hunger for God, and keeps doors half-open that we were meant to walk through. God's invitation is not to hurry; it is to **heed**. If you know "later" has cost you, whisper, *No more delay.*

PERSONAL STORY

For four years, I waited for a man to make room for me; after his kids graduated, after the business sold, after work slowed. The milestones came; the commitment did not. One day, the Holy Spirit whispered, *"This is how you treat Me; you want Me, but you don't make room."*

After four years of waiting for a commitment that never came, God revealed to me that I was asking a man to make room while I had not truly made room for **Him**. I kept saying, "After this season… after this milestone," and my purpose stayed parked.

What I learned is this: even in my delay, God never left me; He stood at the door and waited for me to open it (Hebrews 13:5; Revelation 3:20).

THE STORY

Picture a guest at your front door. He knocks; you hear Him. But you keep cleaning; "Just a minute… after this email… once I finish this call." He waits on the porch while life bustles inside. In the same way, Jesus knocks. The issue is not whether He is near; it is whether we **open**.

THE POINT

In the Parable of the Great Banquet (Luke 14:16-24), the table is set, and the servant says, "Come, for everything is now ready." One by one, the guests send regrets. I bought a field. I am testing my oxen. I just got married. None of it is evil, but normal life becomes a closed door to a holy invitation. The master does not move the feast to a later date. He opens the guest list until the house is full.

That is the heart check Haggai gives: "Give careful thought to your ways" (Haggai 1:5-7). We polish our own houses while God's work waits.

Paul tells the church at Corinth, "Do not receive God's grace in vain… now is the day of salvation" (2 Corinthians 6:1-2). Jesus is at the door, and He is knocking (Revelation 3:20). God is not withholding. We are delaying. Let's clear the excuses and say yes today.

TRANSITION TO CORE TEACHING

How do we move from "later" to "now"? The DELAY principle outlines five steps you can start today.

CORE TEACHING — THE D.E.L.A.Y. PRINCIPLE

D - Decide today, not "someday." "Now is the day of salvation." (2 Corinthians 6:2)

E - End the excuses. "They all alike began to make excuses." (Luke 14:18)

L - Let God be first. "Seek first his Kingdom and his righteousness." (Matthew 6:33)

A - Align your steps with wisdom. "Be very careful… making the most of every opportunity." (Ephesians 5:15-16)

Y - Yield the outcome to God. "Wait for the LORD; be strong and take heart." (Psalm 27:14)

Before you move, listen. Let the Spirit put His finger on where delay has lived in your life.

REFLECTION QUESTIONS

1. Where have I been saying "later" to God, and what has that delay cost me?

2. Which excuse do I use most often—and what truth from God replaces it?

3. What would "seek first" look like in my calendar this week?

4. What single act of obedience can I do in the next 24 hours?

5. What outcome do I need to **yield** rather than control?

Turn reflection into rhythm. Practice these small, steady yeses for the next 30 days.

MONTHLY CHALLENGE

For the next 30 days

- Give God the **first 15** (minutes) daily in the Word, prayer, and a written "one next step."

- Replace one chronic excuse with a **daily micro-yes** (10-minute action toward your calling).

- **Time-block** one hour weekly for Kingdom assignment (serve, create, study, or mentor).

CLOSING SCRIPTURES TO MEDITATE ON

"Seek first his Kingdom and his righteousness…" (Matthew 6:33)

"Here I am! I stand at the door and knock…" (Revelation 3:20)

"Commit to the LORD whatever you do, and he will establish your plans." (Proverbs 16:3)

TAKE IT FURTHER

- Memorize 2 Corinthians 6:2 and use it as your "no-delay" alarm.
- Share your next step with an accountability partner and check in weekly.
- Create a simple "God-first" routine card (Scripture, prayer line, next step) and tape it where you start your day.

D.E.L.A.Y. Principle

This is where what you have read becomes how you live. Over the next four weeks, record your wins as proof of God's work in and through you.

Small victories build lasting transformation. Recording them creates a testimony you can return to for encouragement. Each week, note progress in the Reflection, Challenge, and Take It Further activities.

This month, I commit to living out **D.E.L.A.Y.** (Decide Today-Not "Someday", End the Excuses, Let God Be First, Align Your Steps with Wisdom, Yield the Outcome to God).

Signature: _____ Date: _____

WEEK 1:

Reflection Question Win: _____

30-Day Challenge Win: _____

Take It Further Win: _____

WEEK 2:

Reflection Question Win: _____

30-Day Challenge Win: _____

Take It Further Win: _____

WEEK 3:

Reflection Question Win: _____

30-Day Challenge Win: _____

Take It Further Win: _____

WEEK 4:

Reflection Question Win: _____

30-Day Challenge Win: _____

Take It Further Win: _____

Chapter Nine

We have talked about ending the delay—removing the "not yet" that keeps God waiting. But once you have said "yes" to moving forward, the question becomes: Which way now? Sometimes the next step is not a giant leap; it is a simple shift in posture, attention, or obedience. In the next chapter, we will see how one small move—one letter's difference—can completely change your direction.

 Scan the QR Code or enter the link to listen to the audio message.

https://youtu.be/Dw62FdNb7LQ

9

The Shift: When One Letter Can Make a Difference

One letter. One move. One divine difference.

Scripture Focus: 1 Samuel 3:1-10 (NIV); Psalm 46:10 (NIV); Proverbs 3:5-6 (NIV); Isaiah 30:21 (NIV)

OPENING TRANSITION

Sometimes the biggest changes in our lives begin with the smallest movements - a single step, a fresh word, a shift. Just like changing one letter can turn "here" into "there," or "there" into "where," one act of obedience can transform your direction and destiny. Today, we learn to shift toward God's voice.

OPENING PRAYER

Lord, thank You for speaking, whether through whispers, nudges, or clear instructions. Help me to quiet the noise, lean in close, and recognize Your voice. Give me the courage to make the small shifts that align me with Your will. In Jesus' name, Amen.

INTRODUCTION

We often look for God in big signs, a booming voice, a miraculous door flung wide. But more often, His guidance comes as a gentle invitation to move one step closer. That is how it happened to Samuel.

In 1 Samuel 3, the boy Samuel served in the temple under Eli. He heard a voice calling his name and thought it was Eli. Three times he ran to Eli, only to learn it was God calling. One small change, saying, "Speak, Lord, for Your servant is listening," shifted Samuel from hearing without understanding to hearing with obedience. That shift did not just change his night; it shaped his life.

PERSONAL STORY

I remember a time when I kept asking God for "the big answer." I sought clarity on my next steps in work, ministry, and relationships. I prayed, but I wasn't truly listening; I was waiting for confirmation that matched my expectations. One day during my quiet time, I felt God nudge me: "The answer is already in what I have told you. You just have not acted on it."

I realized I did not need a whole new plan. I just needed to shift one conversation, one change in my schedule, one "yes" I had been holding back. That tiny move opened the door for the bigger changes I had been praying for all along.

THE STORY

Samuel's shift was not about location; it was about posture. He was already in the right place; he just needed to be in the right position to listen. When he said, "Speak, Lord," it was like turning the radio dial until the static cleared. Suddenly, God's message came through loud and clear.

THE POINT

God's direction often comes in the middle of our routine. The difference between staying where you are and stepping into where God wants you is not always dramatic; it is usually a small but deliberate shift. That is why this month's teaching is built on the SHIFT principle.

TRANSITION TO CORE TEACHING

If we want to see change in our lives, we must start with intentional, faith-driven steps. The SHIFT principle serves as your guide, breaking down how to position yourself to hear, respond, and move when God speaks.

CORE TEACHING — THE S.H.I.F.T. PRINCIPLE

S – Seek: God's presence where you are. "Seek the LORD while he may be found; call on him while he is near." (Isaiah 55:6)

H – Hear: His voice through prayer and stillness. "Be still and know that I am God." (Psalm 46:10)

I – Identify: His direction for your life. "Whether you turn to the right or to the left, your ears will hear a voice… saying, 'This is the way; walk in it." (Isaiah 30:21)

F – Follow: His instructions in obedience. "Do not merely listen to the word… Do what it says." (James 1:22)

T – Trust: His timing when the "where" is not yet clear. "Trust in the LORD… and he will make your paths straight." (Proverbs 3:5-6)

These questions will help you pinpoint where one small step could open the way to greater alignment with Him.

REFLECTION QUESTIONS

1. **Seek:** How am I currently making space for God's presence each day?

2. **Hear:** What distractions keep me from hearing His voice clearly?

3. **Identify:** What area of my life do I sense God is trying to redirect?

4. **Follow:** What one act of obedience have I been delaying that I can take now?

5. **Trust:** Where am I struggling to trust God's timing?

MONTHLY CHALLENGE

For the Next 30 Days

Over the next month, make three intentional shifts in your walk with God:

- Daily Quiet Time: Set aside at least 10 minutes each day for un-interrupted prayer or Scripture reading.

- Obedience Step: Act on one thing God has already told you to do, no matter how small.

- Weekly Reflection: Journal one way each week that you have seen God move because you shifted your mindset, habits, or priorities.

CLOSING SCRIPTURES TO MEDITATE

"Speak, for your servant is listening." (1 Samuel 3:10)

"Be still and know that I am God." (Psalm 46:10)

"Trust in the LORD with all your heart..." (Proverbs 3:5-6)

TAKE IT FURTHER

- Memorize 1 Samuel 3:10 as a daily listening prayer.
- Ask a trusted friend to be your "SHIFT partner." Share one step you will take this week and check in together.
- Choose one area of your life where you will intentionally swap busyness for stillness with God.

S.H.I.F.T. Principle

This is where what you have read becomes how you live. Over the next four weeks, record your wins as proof of God's work in and through you.

Small victories build lasting transformation. Recording them creates a testimony you can return to for encouragement. Each week, note progress in the Reflection, Challenge, and Take It Further activities.

This month, I commit to living out **S.H.I.F.T.** (Seek God's Presence, Here His Voice, Identify His Direction, Follow His Instructions, Trust His Timing).

Signature: _____ Date: _____

WEEK 1:

Reflection Question Win: _____

30-Day Challenge Win: _____

Take It Further Win: _____

WEEK 2:

Reflection Question Win: _____

30-Day Challenge Win: _____

Take It Further Win: _____

WEEK 3:

Reflection Question Win: _____

30-Day Challenge Win: _____

Take It Further Win: _____

WEEK 4:

Reflection Question Win: _____

30-Day Challenge Win: _____

Take It Further Win: _____

Chapter Ten

We see how a simple shift in posture, attention, or obedience can completely change your direction. The next chapter encourages you to walk in the direction that God has prepared.

 Scan the QR Code or enter the link to listen to the audio message.

https://youtu.be/Gw3JPnJlpi8

CHAPTER

10

The PATH: Jesus Cleared the Way

*Be encouraged, stay faithful, and keep
walking the PATH He prepared.*

Scripture Focus: Isaiah 45:2 (NIV); Psalm 32:8 (NIV); Proverbs 3:5-6
(NIV); Romans 15:13 (NIV); Exodus 14:21-22 (NIV)

OPENING TRANSITION

Before we take a single step, Jesus has already gone ahead of us. He clears
obstacles we do not even see and prepares the way so we can walk safely
into His promises. Just like a father making sure the trail is clear for his
child, our Savior removes dangers, directs our steps, and leads us forward
with love. Today, we walk the path knowing He has already made the way.

OPENING PRAYER

Lord Jesus, thank You for going before me. Thank You for preparing my
steps, for removing obstacles I cannot see, and for leading me toward Your
perfect will. Help me to trust Your guidance, rest in Your assurance, and
walk with hope. In Your name - Amen.

INTRODUCTION

In Exodus 14, the Israelites stood trapped with an impossible sea before them and Pharaoh's army behind them. But God told Moses to stretch out his hand, and the waters parted. The path was not visible until God made a way.

We often think walking with God means forging our own way forward. But more often, He calls us to follow a path. He has already cleared. One we could never create ourselves. The challenge is to trust Him enough to step into it.

PERSONAL STORY

One morning on my walk, I saw a father jogging ahead of his young son. The boy was close behind; his eyes fixed on the trail. Up ahead, a section of wire fencing had fallen across the path. Without hesitation, the father stopped, pulled the fencing aside, and made sure the way was safe before continuing.

In that moment, I thought, "This is exactly how Jesus goes ahead of me." I often only notice the smooth trail, not realizing how many obstacles He has already removed. He does not just point us in the right direction; He ensures the path is safe enough for us to follow.

THE STORY

When God parted the Red Sea, He did not just make a narrow walkway. Scripture says the Israelites crossed on dry ground. The Lord did not leave them trudging through mud; He made the way firm beneath their feet.

Jesus does the same in our lives. He clears the way, prepares our steps, and ensures we can move forward in His strength, not just barely making it, but walking securely.

THE POINT

God is not only a way-maker; He is a path-preparer. Before you even face tomorrow, He has already been there removing obstacles, arranging divine appointments, and setting your feet on solid ground. That is why this month's principle is built on the path. He does not just show you the way, He is the way.

TRANSITION TO CORE TEACHING

If you want to walk in the fullness of what God has for you, you must follow the path, living with the confidence that Jesus has already prepared the road ahead. The PATH principle gives us four practical ways to walk with purpose.

CORE TEACHING — THE P.A.T.H. PRINCIPLE

P – Preparation: Jesus prepares the way ahead of us.

"I will go before you and will level the mountains; I will break down gates of bronze and cut through bars of iron." (Isaiah 45:2)

A – Assurance: We have the assurance that He will guide us.

"I will instruct you and teach you in the way you should go; I will counsel you with my loving eye on you." (Psalm 32:8)

T – Trust: We are called to trust His direction completely.

"Trust in the LORD with all your heart and lean not on your own under-standing; in all your ways submit to him, and he will make your P.A.T.H.s straight." (Proverbs 3:5-6)

H – Hope: We move forward with hope in His promises.

"May the God of hope fill you with all joy and peace as you trust in him, so that you may overflow with hope by the power of the Holy Spirit." (Romans 15:13)

Walking the path is more than knowing the steps; it is about living them daily.

Reflection helps us pause, look at where we are, and notice how God is actively guiding us. Let these questions help you see where you are already on the path, and where you might need to realign your steps with His.

REFLECTION QUESTIONS

1. **Preparation** - Where have I seen God prepare a way for me before I even took the first step?

2. **Assurance** - How has God's guidance been clear in my life recently?

3. **Trust** - What step have I been afraid to take that requires trusting Him fully?

4. **Hope** - In what area of my life do I need fresh hope today?

5. How can I follow Jesus' lead more closely instead of trying to create my own path?

Reflection opens our eyes, but action moves our feet. Once we have identified where God is speaking, we take intentional steps to walk that path with Him.

This month's challenge will help you practice the P.ATH principle in tangible ways.

MONTHLY CHALLENGE

For the next 30 days

- Daily Gratitude Walk: Each day, thank Jesus for at least one "cleared PATH" you notice.

- Faith Step: Act on one thing God has been prompting you to do, even if the way forward is not fully clear.

- Weekly Reflection: Journal one situation each week where you experienced His preparation, assurance, trust, or hope.

CLOSING SCRIPTURES TO MEDITATE ON

"I will go before you and will level the mountains..." (Isaiah 45:2)

"I will instruct you and teach you in the way you should go..." (Psalm 32:8)

"Trust in the LORD with all your heart..." (Proverbs 3:5-6)

TAKE IT FURTHER

- Memorize Isaiah 45:2 as a reminder of God's preparation.
- Share a testimony with someone about a time God cleared the way for you.
- Spend one hour this month in an uninterrupted quiet with God, asking Him to show you the next step on your PATH.

P.A.T.H. Principle

This is where what you have read becomes how you live. Over the next four weeks, record your wins as proof of God's work in and through you.

Small victories build lasting transformation. Recording them creates a testimony you can return to for encouragement. Each week, note progress in the Reflection, Challenge, and Take It Further activities.

This month, I commit to living out **P.A.T.H.** (Preparation, Assurance, Trust, and Hope).

Signature: _____ Date: _____

WEEK 1:

Reflection Question Win: _____

30-Day Challenge Win: _____

Take It Further Win: _____

WEEK 2:

Reflection Question Win: _____

30-Day Challenge Win: _____

Take It Further Win: _____

WEEK 3:

Reflection Question Win: _____

30-Day Challenge Win: _____

Take It Further Win: _____

WEEK 4:

Reflection Question Win: _____

30-Day Challenge Win: _____

Take It Further Win: _____

Chapter Eleven

Once you are walking the path Jesus has cleared, the journey is not just about moving forward; it is about how you travel along the way. Even on the right path, we can move so fast that we forget to stop. In this next section, we will learn why sometimes the most powerful thing we can do is pause and breathe in God's presence. That is where the PAUSE comes in.

 Scan the QR Code or enter the link to listen to the audio message.

https://youtu.be/8o2gM6s_JkM

11

Pause: Do not Forget to Breathe

*Sometimes the most powerful act of faith
is to simply pause and breathe.*

Scripture Focus: Luke 10:38-42 (The story of Mary and Martha)

OPENING TRANSITION

As we step into this chapter, I want to invite you to reflect on a moment we often overlook: the simple act of pausing to breathe. Just as we need to breathe physically, we need to pause spiritually. Let's explore how Jesus' visit with Mary and Martha shows us the beauty of choosing to sit at His feet, even when life is busy.

OPENING PRAYER

Heavenly Father, as we begin this chapter, we ask for Your presence to fill our hearts. Help us to pause, to breathe, and to truly listen for Your voice. May we learn from Your Word and be reminded that our relationship with You is not about constant activity, but about resting in Your presence. In Jesus' name, Amen.

INTRODUCTION

The pace of life today is fast, and even in our faith, we can become so focused on doing for God that we forget to simply be with Him. This is not a modern problem; Martha faced it too. Her desire to serve Jesus was genuine, but it kept her from enjoying His company.

The lesson? Spiritual strength does not come from constant motion. It comes from stillness, from being available to breathe in God's presence before moving forward.

PERSONAL STORY

I work out with a wonderful personal trainer in his eighties, and he always reminds me of one simple yet crucial truth: **never forget to breathe**. In the middle of a workout, when I am focused on my form and effort, he will say: "Inhale, exhale, let your breath guide you." It is amazing how something so basic can be so easy to forget when we are in motion.

Spiritually, we can be the same way. Life's responsibilities and demands can leave us breathless, not because we are not capable, but because we forget to pause in God's presence. That is exactly what is revealed in the story of Mary and Martha.

THE STORY (MARY AND MARTHA)

In Luke 10:38-42, Jesus visits the home of two sisters. Martha is busy preparing the meal and tending to tasks, while Mary simply sits at Jesus' feet, listening. When Martha asks Jesus to tell Mary to help, He gently reminds her that Mary has chosen the better part, being present with Him.

THE POINT

We often live like Martha, doing so many good things that we forget the best thing: being still with Jesus. Jesus' words remind us that pausing to be in His presence is never wasted time.

CORE TEACHING: THE P.A.U.S.E. PRINCIPLE

P - Pray and center yourself in God's presence. (Philippians 4:6)

A - Acknowledge your need to slow down. (Psalm 46:10)

U - Unplug from distractions. (Mark 6:31)

S - Sit with Scripture and listen for God's voice. (Psalm 119:105)

E - Exhale and embrace His peace. (John 14:27)

Practicing PAUSE is like spiritual breathing; it restores strength, clarity, and peace.

REFLECTION QUESTIONS

1. When was the last time you truly paused to sit in God's presence?

2. Which part of the PAUSE principle is most challenging for you, and why?

3. How can you create a daily rhythm that includes moments of spiritual "breathing"?

4. Recall a time when being still brought you peace? What happened?

5. What is one area of life where you can slow down and invite God to lead?

MONTHLY CHALLENGE

For the next 30 days

- Set aside at least five minutes daily to practice PAUSE.

- Choose a verse to meditate on, unplug from distractions, and notice how God's peace meets you in the quiet.

CLOSING SCRIPTURES TO MEDITATE ON

"God keeps in perfect peace those who trust Him." (Isaiah 26:3)

"Jesus gives rest to the weary." (Matthew 11:28-29)

"True rest is found in God alone." (Psalm 62:1)

TAKE IT FURTHER

- Find a quiet moment today, even just five minutes and reflect on how pausing shifts your perspective.
- Journal your thoughts and write down one commitment to practice the PAUSE principle this week. Let it be the start of a habit that keeps you spiritually refreshed.

P.A.U.S.E. Principle

This is where what you have read becomes how you live. Over the next four weeks, record your wins as proof of God's work in and through you.

Small victories build lasting transformation. Recording them creates a testimony you can return to for encouragement. Each week, note progress in the Reflection, Challenge, and Take It Further activities.

This month, I commit to living out **P.A.U.S.E.** (Pray, Acknowledge, Unplug, Sit, and Exhale).

Signature: _____ Date: _____

WEEK 1:

Reflection Question Win: _____

30-Day Challenge Win: _____

Take It Further Win: _____

WEEK 2:

Reflection Question Win: _____

30-Day Challenge Win: _____

Take It Further Win: _____

WEEK 3:

Reflection Question Win: _____

30-Day Challenge Win: _____

Take It Further Win: _____

WEEK 4:

Reflection Question Win: _____

30-Day Challenge Win: _____

Take It Further Win: _____

Chapter Twelve

When you pause and breathe in God's presence, you discover more than peace; you discover power. And with that power comes a choice: to stay where you are or to step fully into the freedom He has been preparing for you all along. In this closing chapter, we bring the entire journey together. It is time to put on the armor, embrace your calling, and Escape from Within.

 Scan the QR Code or enter the link to listen to the audio message.

https://youtu.be/5na-cSLqbUI

CHAPTER

12

Escape From Within: Clothed for Victory

*You're not fighting for victory—
you're fighting from it.*

Scripture Focus: "Put on the full armor of God, so that you can take your stand against the devil's schemes." Ephesians 6:11 (NIV)

Additional Scriptures: Galatians 5:1 John 8:36 (NIV)

OPENING TRANSITION

After learning to pause and breathe in God's presence, you now stand in a place of renewed strength, clarity, and readiness. Every chapter before this has been a step in a greater journey, not just to change what is around you, but to transform what is within you. And now, it is time to step fully into freedom. This closing chapter is your commissioning moment. This is where you *Escape from Within*.

OPENING PRAYER

Lord, thank You for walking with me through every chapter of this journey. Thank You for the shifts, the mending, the delays that became divine timing, and the paths You cleared. Today, I put on the full armor You have given me. I stand in freedom, I stand in faith, and I stand ready to walk boldly into the calling You have prepared. Seal this work in my heart and let my life be a testimony of Your power to set the captive free. In Jesus' name - Amen.

INTRODUCTION

Freedom does not begin with a change in our surroundings; it begins with a change in our spirit. The enemy would love us to believe that freedom is impossible, that we will always be bound by fear, doubt, or the wounds of our past. But the truth is, Jesus came to set us free from the inside out.

When Paul wrote to the church in Ephesus about putting on the armor of God, he was not just talking about protection; he was talking about preparation. God does not only want you safe from attack; He wants you equipped for victory.

PERSONAL STORY

For years, I lived my faith like I was outside of a prison cell, but still holding the keys in my hand, unsure how to use them. I could quote scripture, pray powerful prayers, and serve faithfully, but inside, I was still carrying chains of insecurity, disappointment, and fear of the unknown.

God began to show me that my greatest escape would not be from my circumstances, but from the limits I had placed in my own heart. Through each principle in this book (DRIVE, FUEL, OPEN, ALARM, FAITH, FATHER, MEND, DELAY, SHIFT, PAUSE), I was not just learning steps to live better; I was learning how to live free.

And now, I can stand here and say, I am on a continuous journey to escape from within.

THE POINT

This is not just the end of a book; it is the start of your commission. You have been equipped with every tool you need to stand against the enemy and walk boldly in your God-given purpose. Freedom is not a destination; it is a way of living. And every day you choose to put on God's armor, you choose to live that freedom out loud.

TRANSITION TO CORE TEACHING:

Every chapter you have walked through has been a piece of your spiritual escape plan. But God does not just want you to experience a breakthrough once; He wants you to live it daily. That is why this final principle, ESCAPE, weaves together everything we have learned into one powerful, God-centered lifestyle. Each letter is more than a step; it is a way of living in the freedom Christ secured for you.

CORE TEACHING - THE E.S.C.A.P.E. PRINCIPLE

E - Engage Your Calling (God's First Choice: DRIVE principle): You were chosen before you even took your first breath. Step into it boldly.

S - Stay Fueled in Faith (Lift the Nozzle: FUEL principle): Never let your spiritual tank run dry. Keep your worship, prayer, and Word intake strong.

C - Connect to God's Voice (Muted Lines, Open Heaven: OPEN principle): Silence the noise so you can hear His clear instructions.

A - Awaken to Your Assignment (Wake Up: ALARM principle): Be alert. Live ready. Your obedience can change lives.

P - Persevere in Purpose (FAITH, MEND, DELAY, SHIFT, PATH, PAUSE): Stay the course when it is hard, trust the timing, and embrace the changes.

E - Embrace God's Armor: Stand firm. You are not just surviving anymore; you are advancing. (Ephesians 6:11)

REFLECTION QUESTIONS

1. Which principle from this journey has impacted your life the most?

2. What area of your life still needs an "escape" from "within"?

3. How will you live differently now that you understand freedom is yours in Christ?

MONTHLY CHALLENGE

For the next 30 days

Intentionally live out one letter of ESCAPE each week. By the end, you will have reinforced every principle and strengthened your walk in freedom.

CLOSING SCRIPTURES TO MEDITATE ON

"Put on the full armor of God, so that you can take your stand against the devil's schemes." (Ephesians 6:11)

"It is for freedom that Christ has set us free..." (Galatians 5:1)

"So, if the Son sets you free, you will be free indeed." (John 8:36)

FINAL CHARGE

Your journey to *Escape from Within* is not about running away; it is about stepping fully into who God created you to be. Go live free. Go live boldly. And never forget, the same God who set you free will keep you free.

Transition to Bonus Chapter & Next Series Divine Detours

*As we come to the close of **Escape from Within**, think of this moment not as an ending but as the threshold of a new journey. The bonus chapter you are about to read is a glimpse into my next series, **Divine Detours**.*

In Divine Detours, we will dive into how God's surprising redirections can actually be His way of lovingly guiding us. The first chapter of this new journey, 'When the AC Fails, Trust God's Direction,' offers a glimpse into the powerful lessons ahead, demonstrating that even life's detours can be divine opportunities for growth.

If you have found hope in Escape from Within, get ready to embrace the adventure that Divine Detours will bring. Let's step forward together into the next 12 months of discovering how God's redirections are always covered in His grace.

Divine Detours: When the AC Fails, Trust God's Redirection

GOD SOMETIMES BLOCKS TO PROTECT

Our action for this month is Discern.

Scripture Focus: "The angel of the Lord asked him, 'Why have you beaten your donkey these three times? I have come here to oppose you because your path is a reckless one before me.'" Numbers 22:32 (NIV)

OPENING TRANSITION

Sometimes God's guidance shows up in the most unexpected ways. We might think we have everything planned out, but He sees the bigger picture. Let's open in prayer, and then I will share how a little AC trouble turned into a big reminder of God's protection.

OPENING PRAYER

Dear Lord, we thank You for Your guidance and for the ways You watch over us, even when we don't see it right away. We ask that you open our hearts to understand the lessons you place before us and to trust that your path is always for our good. In Jesus' name, Amen.

INTRODUCTION

What if the thing that breaks is actually what saves you?

So often, we view inconvenience as a setback. But what if it's a setup? A pause? A holy intervention? That is what I came to understand when a routine visit turned into a divine detour, thanks to a broken AC unit.

PERSONAL STORY

Let me tell you what happened.

I invited someone I had been casually dating long-distance for over four years to stay over. He usually stays in a hotel, but I have a spare room since my daughter moved out. We thought it would be a simple visit, nothing out of the ordinary. But just as he was on his way, my air conditioner, which had been working perfectly fine, suddenly stopped. The heat was unbearable. He decided to go to a hotel instead.

At first, I was frustrated. It felt like such bad timing. But the longer I sat with it, the more I realized: this was **God stepping in**. He blocked something I did not need to walk into.

The AC did not fail. It functioned as divine protection. A holy interruption.

THE STORY – (BALAAM AND THE DONKEY)

This made me think of Balaam in Numbers 22.

Balaam was headed down a road he thought was right. But his donkey kept stopping. What Balaam did not realize was that the **Angel of the Lord** was standing in the path, sword drawn, ready to oppose him.

God used a donkey to protect him.

Sometimes we are so determined to go our own way that we miss the warning signs. And sometimes, God will use something as simple as a broken appliance or a silent "no" to block us from disaster.

THE POINT

I thought I was in control. But God was showing me that His plan over-rules mine every time. What looked like an inconvenience was a **divine detour.**

TRANSITION TO CORE TEACHING

That is when I heard it clearly in my spirit: **"You are Always Covered."**

CORE TEACHING - THE A.C. PRINCIPLE:

A.C. equals Always Covered

- Even when life does not go according to plan…

- Even when things break down…

- Even when people let you down…

- Even when it feels unfair or uncomfortable…

You Are Still Always Covered by God's Protection.

God does not just open doors. He closes them too. And the closed ones often protect us more than we realize.

REFLECTION QUESTIONS

1. Can you recall a time when an unexpected inconvenience might have been God protecting you?

2. How can you become more aware of God's guidance in your everyday life?

3. What does being 'Always Covered' by God's protection mean to you personally?

4. Are there areas where you need to trust that God might be blocking something for your own good?

5. How can you apply this idea of God's protective 'AC' in your life right now?

MONTHLY CHALLENGE

This month, I invite you to reflect on a situation where things didn't go as planned. Was it a breakdown? A delay? A shift? Consider how it might have been God's way of redirecting you. Write it down, pray about it, and **thank Him for His protection, even if you did not see it at the time.**

CLOSING SCRIPTURES TO MEDITATE ON

"The Lord will keep you from all harm; He will watch over your life; the Lord will watch over your coming and going both now and forevermore." (Psalm 121:7-8)

"In their hearts humans plan their course, but the Lord establishes their steps." (Proverbs 16:9)

TAKE IT FURTHER:

This was just one of many divine detours I have experienced. And every one of them was God's way of guiding me toward His best. That is why I am inviting you to join me on my next devotional journey: **Divine Detours.**

Because sometimes the roadblock is the blessing.

What's Next

DIVINE DETOURS: TRUSTING GOD'S REDIRECTION THROUGH EVERY SEASON (NEW SERIES)

When plans fall apart, heaven may be stepping in.

Divine Detours helps you reframe life's interruptions as God's loving redirections. The bonus chapter you just read, *When the AC Fails, Trust God's Redirection*, sets the tone: what "breaks" may actually be what saves you, because you are **Always Covered**.

God does not just open doors; He closes them, too. This series will help you notice those moments, trust His guidance, and move forward in faith.

Inside the series:

- Personal and biblical stories of detours that became blessings.
- The **A.C. principle** (e.g., Always Covered, Always Called) in each chapter, grounded in scripture and reflection.
- Monthly actions and faith steps to help you follow God's lead with purpose and peace.

Your Next Step:

Invite a friend or small group to join you. Start with the bonus chapter and reflect on one "holy interruption" God used in your life this month. What if the detour was divine?

A Week of Walking
(5-Day Devotional)

Turn everyday steps into worship, reflection, and growth. This pocket-sized journey combines short readings, prayers, declarations, and audio that you can listen to while walking (QR codes/links included). Topics include **Walking in Wisdom, Walking Worthy, Walking in the Word, Walking to Win,** and **Walking into the Next**.

Perfect next step after this book:

- Take 5 days to reset your pace with God.

- Use the built-in audio during your daily walk.

- Close the week with a simple "Your Next Step" plan and share your testimony.

About the Author

Ratondrea O'Neal is the founder of From Within Inspirations LLC and the creator of 3AM Breakthroughs, short late-night audio reflections that offer hope, strength, and spiritual clarity. A Certified Learning Engineer and mother, she writes devotionals for adults and teens that help readers trust God and take simple daily steps toward breakthrough. She holds a BA in Sociology from the University of South Florida, an MS in Organizational Performance and Workplace E-Learning, and a Graduate Certificate in Workplace E-Learning and Performance Support from Boise State University. Her mission is to help readers trust God and take one small step at a time toward spiritual breakthrough. Through her writing and audio, she invites you to Escape From Within and live with steady hope.

References & Attributions

STORIES & ILLUSTRATIONS

"The Bird and the Snow" - Adapted from a traditional moral story, author unknown.